mat. # 800062

J
B
GRI

12,458

W9-BDM-608

Jam Session

Ken Griffey, Jr.

Terri Dougherty
ABDO Publishing Company

visit us at
www.abdopub.com

Published by ABDO Publishing Company, 4940 Viking Drive, Suite 622, Edina, Minnesota 55435. Copyright © 2001 by Abdo Consulting Group, Inc. International copyrights reserved in all countries. No part of this book may be reproduced in any form without written permission from the publisher.

Printed in the United States.

Cover and Interior Photo credits: AP Wide World Photos; All-Sport Photos

Edited by Denis Dougherty

Book design: Patrick Laurel

Sources: Associated Press; Newsweek; New York Daily News; People Magazine; Sports Illustrated; Sports Illustrated For Kids; Time Magazine; ESPN Magazine; USA Today

Library of Congress Cataloging-in-Publication Data

Dougherty, Terri.
    Ken Griffey, Jr. / Terri Dougherty.
        p.   cm. -- (Jam Session)
    Includes index.
     ISBN 1-57765-472-2
    1. Griffey, Ken, Jr.--Juvenile literature. 2. Baseball players--United States--Biography--
Juvenile literature. [1. Griffey, Ken, Jr. 2. Baseball players. 3. Afro-Americans--Biography]
    I. Title. II. Series.

    GV865.G69 D68 2001
    796.357'092--dc21
    [B]   00-048527

Contents

Family Fun

*W*hen Ken Griffey, Jr. smacked a 2-0 pitch from Rolando Arrojo into the left-field seats at Coors Field in Denver, he made history. On April 10, 2000, the hard-hitting Cincinnati Reds center fielder known as Junior became the youngest player to hit 400 home runs. He was moving closer to breaking Hank Aaron's career record of 755.

The crowd cheered as Junior rounded the bases. When he entered the Reds' dugout, his dad was waiting there to give him a hug. "It's a special moment for both of us, especially that I can do that in front of him," Junior said.

The home run was a special birthday present for Junior's dad, Ken Griffey, Sr. It was just one of the many exciting moments the father and son have shared on the baseball field. Ken Sr. is a coach for the Reds. He played in the major leagues for 19 seasons. He was a key part of the Reds teams that won the World Series in 1975 and 1976. But he says the highlight of his career was playing alongside Junior for the Seattle Mariners in 1990 and 1991.

"The time I played with him was special; it was emotional for me," Ken Sr. said. "On the field I was his teammate, off the field I was his father, and on the bench I was his coach."

Ken Sr. may have his World Series rings, but his son is a superstar in his own right. Junior's quick bat, power, and thrilling catches in the outfield make him one of the top players of all time. His outstanding play in the outfield earned him 10 Gold Gloves while he was with the Mariners. He's been the top All-Star Game vote-getter five times, and was the 1997 American League MVP. He was voted the Players Choice Player of the Decade for the 1990s.

"Growing up, my dad always told me, 'Have fun. Don't worry if you make an out,' " Junior recalled. " 'Just do the best job you can.' "

**Ken Griffey, Sr. (left) congratulates his son,
Ken Griffey, Jr. after a Reds victory.**

Growing up with the 'Big Red Machine'

*J*unior and Senior were both born in Donora, Pennsylvania. Junior's father and mother, Alberta, or "Birdie," met in high school. Both were good athletes. They married after high school. Junior was born on November 21, 1969, six months after Ken Sr. started playing ball in the Reds' minor-league system. Junior's brother, Craig, was born in 1971, and his sister, Lathesia, was born in 1972.

"The days in the minor leagues were the best times because that's when I developed a closeness with them," Ken Sr. said. "I was always with them. I had them all the time."

When Junior was five, his dad became the Reds' regular right fielder. The family moved to Cincinnati. To Junior, it seemed normal to have a dad who was a great ballplayer.

"He was just my father. I didn't think of him as a big star," Junior said. "When he came home, he was just like any other father coming home. I was like any kid. I wanted to play catch with him. He'd play catch with me and with all the kids in the neighborhood."

Because his dad played for the Reds, Junior got to hang out in the locker room at Riverfront Stadium, now called Cinergy Field. He met "Big Red Machine" stars like Pete Rose, Joe Morgan, Tony Perez, Johnny Bench, George Foster, Dave Concepcion, and Cesar Geronimo. He was so at ease with the superstars that he would play tricks on them.

"I remember Junior running around our clubhouse when he was seven or eight," recalled Bench, the Reds' Hall of Fame catcher. "He used to take hats and bats out of my locker! He just laughed and ran off."

Many kids would be in awe of major-leaguers. For Junior it was routine to be in the locker room with them. "Riverfront was just where my dad worked," Junior said. "I didn't walk around thinking, 'Wow, these are the Cincinnati Reds.' "

His mother remembers Junior admiring the team enough to listen to the games on the radio and learn his father's stats. He wore his dad's baseball caps, but they were too big for him. "The bill would fall down and cover his eyes," Birdie said. "So he started wearing caps backward. That's why he wears his hats backward today."

Junior has been wearing his hat backwards since he was a youngster.

Ken Sr. believes the days Junior spent at the ballpark helped his son as a player. "You watch Pete Rose go out and swing a bat for the enjoyment of it—there was nothing Pete liked more than to swing a bat—so many things Junior saw," Ken Sr. said. "And that's why he likes to play the game."

Junior started playing Little League when he was eight years old. His ability stood out from the beginning. "One day Junior was in center field digging up rocks," said Mark Lewis, an infielder for the Baltimore Orioles who played against Junior in Little League. "He was still digging when the ball was hit his way. He looked up, started running, and caught it. He was awesome."

Ken Sr. would pitch 70-mph fastballs, sliders, curves, and changeups to 12-year-old Junior. He wouldn't tell him which pitch was coming. "The biggest thing with Junior when he got of age was to make him adjust from pitch to pitch," Ken Sr. said. "When he got to 13, I couldn't strike him out, so I knew he was pretty good."

Junior was a pitcher when he was in Little League. He later switched to the outfield. His dad taught him baseball should be fun.

Opposite page: Junior swinging for the fences.

"In Little League, you just want to be out there playing—you could care less about winning or losing. The most important thing was that you got to eat ice cream after the game," Junior said. "Once you get to high school, they make winning and losing a little more important. But you're still just out there having a good time."

Not all Fun and Games

*L*ife got a little tougher for Junior after his father joined the New York Yankees in 1981. Junior didn't get to see him as often, and Junior felt pressure to do well on the baseball field to make his dad proud.

"When I did see him, that's when it was tough on him, because he tried to impress me," Ken Sr. said. "And I told him he never had to impress me. As long as he was happy with what he was doing, I didn't care if he was a garbage man, that was fine with me."

Junior's parents admit they spoiled him. When he was 16, he missed a turn on a dark road and wrecked his first car, a Mercedes Benz. He also got a speeding ticket for going 84 mph. "I didn't mind spoiling him," Ken Sr. said. "A lot of things he did, I didn't get a chance to do them when I was that age."

Junior was great at sports at Cincinnati's Moeller High School. His football team won the state championship his junior year, and he had a shot at playing college football. He starred on the school's baseball team. The area near a Thriftway supermarket well beyond the right-field fence was called "Griffway" because he hit so many balls there.

Junior was so impressive he was the first pick in the 1987 amateur baseball draft. The Seattle Mariners were certain there was no one better.

Junior watches one of his many home runs.

Marvelous Mariner

*J*unior had no doubt his ability would carry him from the minor leagues to the majors in a hurry. He first played in Bellingham, Washington, and used to tell his teammates, "I'll be here one week, then move to San Bernardino (Class A), then Double A the week after that."

Junior didn't go through the system quite that fast, but he did do well. His first minor-league hit was a home run. After the season he was named an All-League outfielder. Baseball America named him the top major-league prospect in the Northwest League.

It was difficult for Junior to adjust to life away from home though. No matter how talented a person is, there is always room for improvement. Junior got tired of being corrected on the ballfield. When he went home after the season, he and his father argued about whether Junior should get his own apartment.

Junior felt so down that he tried to commit suicide in January 1988 by swallowing too many aspirin. He was rushed to the hospital and his life was saved. After that scare, Junior and his father patched things up. They learned to talk through their problems and Junior returned to his true form at the ballpark.

Junior spent one more season in the minor leagues, and in 1989 was invited to spring training with the Mariners. He showed he was ready for the majors by setting spring records for the Mariners with 33 hits, 21 RBI, and a 15-game hitting streak.

When manager Joe Lefebvre told Junior, "You're my starting center fielder," Junior was thrilled. "Those probably are the best words I've ever heard."

Junior began his big-league career at 19 years old. Right away, he showed he belonged. He doubled in his first major-league at-bat. His first swing in Seattle was an opposite-field home run. His father was playing with the Reds that season. Ken Sr. came to see Junior play when his team had a night off.

Junior hit 13 home runs before the All-Star break and hoped to be Rookie of the Year. But he was hurt during part of July and August. After he returned, he tried too hard. "He was trying to catch up with the other Rookie of the Year candidates with one swing," Lefebvre said. "Pretty typical for a 19-year-old kid, really. He lost his poise."

Junior placed third in the Rookie of the Year balloting and finished the season with 16 home runs. But he had only begun to tap his talent. "When he finally buckles down and gets serious about this game, there's no telling what kind of numbers he will put on the board," said Gene Clines, the Mariners' hitting coach.

"I don't think anybody's ever been that good at that age. He's in his own category. He is a natural."

Defense was another of Junior's strong suits. He made stunning catches, such as one that sent him flying over the top of the center-field wall at Yankee Stadium. "I'm in awe," said Ken Sr., who saw the catch when his team had a night off. "Yes, I'm a very proud dad."

"Every time he makes one of those plays, you think he'll never top that one," said Lefebvre. "You can't believe how much it picks up the entire club. He's going to be one of the real marquee players in this league."

Opposite page: Junior is not just an offensive star. Here he shows why he is a yearly Gold Glove winner.

Father-Son Game

*I*n August 1990, the Griffeys got the chance to see a lot more of each other. They became the first father-son duo to play in the majors together. The Griffeys hit back-to-back singles in their first game together. Three weeks later, they homered back to back against the Angels at Anaheim Stadium.

"We could've lost all our games the rest of the season and I wouldn't have cared," Junior said. "We were having such a great time playing together, being teammates, playing baseball."

After injuries forced Ken Sr. to retire after the 1991 season, he became the Mariners' hitting coach in 1993. But he didn't tamper with his son's successful swing. "I haven't bothered with his swing since he was 9 years old," Ken Sr. said.

The Mariners were looking to Junior to lead them to postseason play. The team was formed in 1977, and didn't have a winning season until 1991. Junior kept producing. He led Seattle in every offensive category in 1993. He hit .309 and had an eight-game home run streak.

"He hit some to right, some to left," said Lou Piniella, Mariners' manager at the time. "Not a cheap one in the bunch."

"The thing about Junior, he has that golden smile," said Frank Thomas of the Chicago White Sox. "He is like a kid on the sandlot. We're all competitors, we all play to win, but he always seems to be having more fun than the rest of us."

Junior enjoyed playing ball, but he also learned fame has its price. People called him a pampered prince and were always asking for his autograph. Some fans knocked on his door in the middle of the night. He learned he couldn't please everyone.

Bright spots in Junior's life away from the ballpark were his marriage to Melissa and the birth of their two children. They have a son, Trey Kenneth, born in 1994; and a daughter, Taryn Kennedy born in 1995. "Every day, I pinch myself and say I can't believe I have this great family," Junior said. "You could take away baseball, take away all my material things, but I would still have them. That means everything to me."

The Mariners won their division in 1995 and 1997, but did not reach the World Series. Junior, however, set a record with five home runs against the Yankees in the '95 Division Series. He singled and scored the winning run from first base in the 11th inning of the fifth and deciding game of that series.

Home Runs, and Dreaming of Home

It looked like Junior might add his name to the record books in one more category in 1997 and 1998. He was close to breaking one of baseball's most-treasured records—Roger Maris' record of 61 home runs in a single season. But he always claimed the record wasn't important to him. He'd rather be on a winning team like his father had been.

Junior having fun with his daughter.

Along with Mark McGwire and Sammy Sosa, he got off to a hot home run hitting start in the 1998 season. "Let me ask you something: Where were Mac (McGwire), Sammy (Sosa), and I last October?" he said. "Sitting at home watching the World Series on TV like everybody else. That's all that matters."

In 1998, he joined Babe Ruth and McGwire as the only players with back-to-back 50-homer years. "I've been compared to Willie Mays, Barry Bonds, and many others, but I just have to be the best player that I can be, not what everybody expects me to be," Junior said. "If I feel that I've given 110 percent, I can't worry about what other people think or say. I have two kids at the house I can't cheat. If I cheat myself, then I cheat them. That's motivation for me."

Junior spent 11 seasons in Seattle. He was a 10-time All-Star for the Mariners. He hit 398 home runs there. But he never stopped dreaming of playing in the city he grew up in. "You never stop thinking about it," he said. "You always want to play in front of your hometown fans. That's the ultimate."

Junior and his son take a ride on a roller coaster.

A Red-Letter Trade

*I*n February 2000, Junior's wish came true. He was traded to the Cincinnati Reds. He was excited to be playing at the same stadium he watched his dad play in. He was happy to be close to his grandmother, who used to share stories with him when he was a child. "Every little boy has a dream of playing at home in front of his family and friends, and it was the same with me," Griffey said.

The trade also made it easier for his son and daughter to come to his games. The family lives in Orlando, Florida. "It's a six-hour flight from Orlando to Seattle, and with my kids being involved in summer programs and school, they weren't going to be able to make the flight as often as I would like," he said. "So the move I made allows me to see them more often, and that means more to me than hitting the baseball or running into walls (to make a catch). To be able to run around with them means a lot to me. We're a family that likes to be together."

Junior was given a hero's welcome in Cincinnati. It seemed everyone in the city was wearing something with his name on it. An opening-day parade included a six-foot statue of him. He received a long standing ovation when he was introduced at the ballpark. His dad, a coach for the Reds, got tears in his eyes as he watched from the dugout.

"I knew there would be noise, but I didn't figure it would be that loud, that long," Junior said. "It was a little strange because I didn't know what to expect coming here, but the response was awesome."

"This town has been electrified with the addition of Junior," said Reds manager Jack McKeon. "It's going to be something special."

Junior wears number 30 in Cincinnati, his dad's old number. At Cinergy Field, the second deck in right field is nicknamed "Junior's Playpen" because of the homers he hits there.

Fans expected a lot of Junior during his first season in Cincinnati. But he had a hard time adjusting to the pitchers in the National League. Still, his manager stood behind him. "He's a producer," McKeon said. "He's doing his share."

Fans hope Junior can bring a World Series trophy back to Cincinnati. That's what he hopes, too. "I'm having fun," Junior said. "Just to be in the same locker room as my dad makes me want to do the same things he did as a player. Hopefully, I can win a World Series or two."

Junior admires his first home run hit as a Red.

Ken Griffey, Jr. Profile

Born: November 21, 1969, in
   Donora, Pennsylvania

Height: 6-foot-3

Weight: 205 pounds

Position: Center fielder

Bats: Left

Throws: Left

Resides: Orlando, Florida

Family: Wife, Melissa; son, Trey Kenneth (born January 19, 1994);
   daughter, Taryn Kennedy (born October 21, 1995)

Personal: Following 1993 season, he made his acting debut in the movie "Little Big League" ... Received 1994 Celebrity Recognition Award from the Make-A-Wish Foundation and the A. Bartlett Giamatti Award from the Baseball Assistance Team in recognition of his "caring for fellow citizens" ... Sponsored Christmas dinners for 350 youngsters from the Rainier Vista Boys and Girls Club ... Selected as Mariners' Roberto Clemente Award winner for community service in 1996, '97, and '98 ... Junior's favorite sport to watch other than baseball is basketball ... Likes to play golf and go fishing ... Is neighbors with Tiger Woods and Michael Jordan... Prefers Chinese food ... Admires football and baseball star Deion

Sanders ... Looked up to baseball player Rickey Henderson when he was growing up ... Biggest thrill in sports has been playing for the Mariners with his dad ... When not playing baseball enjoys playing video games with his kids or by himself.

Ken Griffey, Jr. Awards and Honors

Won 10 consecutive Gold Gloves in AL (1990-99)—the longest streak ever among AL outfielders.

Voted to AL's starting lineup in All-Star Game in 10 consecutive seasons (1990-99).

Voted to NL's starting lineup for 2000 All-Star Game, although he did not play because of injury.

Won All-Star Game home run contest three times (1994, 1998, 1999).

Won seven Silver Sluggers (1991, 1993-94, 1996-99) in AL.

All-Star Game MVP (1992).

Won Players Choice Player of the Decade award for the 1990s.

Unanimous choice as AL MVP in 1997.

Player of the Year for his high school league in 1986 and 1987.

Ken Griffey, Jr. Chronology

November 21, 1969 - George Kenneth Griffey, Jr. is born in Donora, Pennsylvania.

1987 - Graduates from Cincinnati's Moeller High School ... Selected by Seattle with the first overall pick in the June baseball draft ... Begins his pro career at age 17 at Bellingham, Washington. ... Named No. 1 major-league prospect in Northwest League by Baseball America.

1988 - Named No. 1 major-league prospect in California League by Baseball America.

1989 - Hits first major-league home run on first pitch he sees at Seattle's Kingdome on April 10 ... Ken Jr. (a member of the Seattle Mariners) and Ken Sr. (a member of the Cincinnati Reds) become first father-son combination to play in majors at same time.

1990 - At age 20, becomes second-youngest player ever to start in an All-Star Game ... On August 31, Ken Jr. and Ken Sr. become first father-son combination to appear in same lineup ... Hits back-to-back homers with Ken Sr. on Sept. 14 ... Becomes second-youngest ever to win a Gold Glove.

1992 - Finishes second among AL outfielders in fielding (.997) ... Named MVP of All-Star Game after going three-for-three with a homer ... Homers and receives MVP honors in the All-Star Game, making the Griffeys the first father and son to accomplish both (Ken Sr. accomplished both feats in 1980).

1993 - Homers in eight straight games to tie major-league record ... Sets AL record for outfielders with 542nd consecutive errorless chance ... Errorless streak ends at 573 chances in 240 games.

1994 - Sets major-league record with 6,079,688 All-Star Game votes.

1995 - Makes great catch crashing into right-center field wall on May 26, but fractures both bones in his left wrist ... Misses 73 games due to injury ... Becomes seventh-youngest player to reach 1,000 hits ... Has outstanding postseason, hitting .364 with six home runs and nine RBI in 11 games ... Singles and scores winning run from first base in 11th inning of decisive fifth game of Division Series ... Ties record for most homers in a postseason series with five in Division Series ... Ties record for most homers in one postseason with six.

1997 - Becomes 13th unanimous MVP selection in baseball history ... Leads majors in RBI, is second in homers, total bases, slugging percentage (.646), and extra-base hits (93) ... Leads AL in runs ... Becomes fourth-youngest player to reach 250 homers despite missing 201 games in his career due to injuries and strikes.

1998 - Becomes second-youngest player to reach 300 homers ... Goes two-for-three and wins home run contest at All-Star Game ... Becomes fourth-youngest player to reach 1,000 RBI ... Becomes third player to have at least 50 homers and 20 stolen bases in a season ... Becomes third player to have at least 140 RBI in three straight seasons ... At age 28, becomes youngest player ever with 350 homers.

1999 - Voted Players Choice Player of the Decade ... Steals career-high 24 bases ... Leads All-Star Game vote-getters for fourth consecutive year and fifth time overall ... Wins All-Star Game home run contest for third time ... Hits 20 homers before June 1 for third time in career (he is the only player to do that) ... Hits seventh opening-day home run of career, tied for second-best in major-league history ... Extends his record among AL outfielders with 10th consecutive Gold Glove ... Finishes 11 seasons with Mariners with .986 fielding percentage.

2000 - On February 10, acquired by the Cincinnati Reds from the Seattle Mariners in exchange for pitchers Brett Tomko and Jake Meyer, outfielder Mike Cameron and infielder Antonio Perez ... Signs contract with Reds through 2008 season with a club option for 2009 ... Leads all major-league outfielders in All-Star Game voting, but does not play in game because of injury ... Gets at least 100 RBI for eighth time.

Junior's Stats

Ken Griffey, Jr.'s Pro Regular Season Batting Statistics

Year	Team	Level	Avg.	HR	RBI
1987	Bellingham (Wash.)	Class A	.313	14	40
1988	San Bernardino (Calif.)	Class A	.338	11	42
1988	Vermont	Class AA	.279	2	10
1989	Seattle	Majors	.264	16	61
1990	Seattle	Majors	.300	22	80
1991	Seattle	Majors	.327	22	100
1992	Seattle	Majors	.308	27	103
1993	Seattle	Majors	.309	45	109
1994	Seattle	Majors	.323	40	90
1995	Seattle	Majors	.258	17	42
1996	Seattle	Majors	.303	49	140
1997	Seattle	Majors	.304	56	147
1998	Seattle	Majors	.284	56	146
1999	Seattle	Majors	.285	48	134
2000	Cincinnati	Majors	.271	40	118

Ken Griffey, Jr.'s Pro Postseason Batting Statistics

Year	Team	Opponent	Level	Avg.	HR	RBI
1995	Seattle	N.Y. Yankees	Division Series	.391	5	7
1995	Seattle	Cleveland	ALCS	.333	1	2
1997	Seattle	Baltimore	Division Series	.133	0	2

KEY:

Avg. - Batting average

HR - Home runs

RBI - Runs batted in

ALCS - American League Championship Series

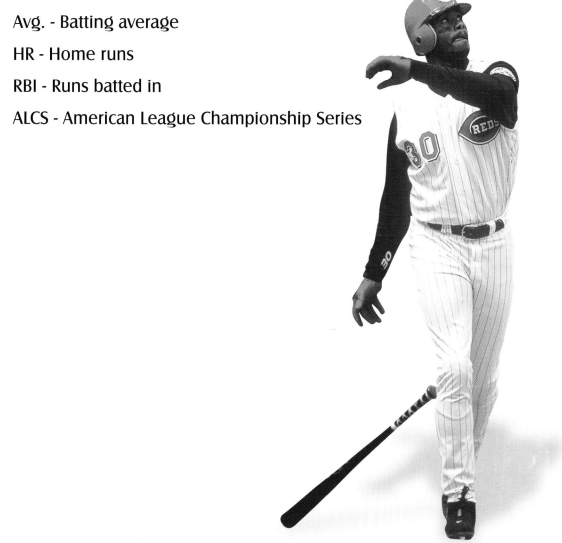

Glossary

AMERICAN LEAGUE – One of the two organizations (along with the National League) that make up Major League Baseball, the highest level of professional baseball.

DEFENSE – The team playing in the field that is trying to keep the opposition from scoring a run.

DIVISION SERIES – A first-round, best-of-five playoff series. The winner advances to the League Championship Series.

DRAFT – A system that gives baseball teams a chance to choose new players.

HOME RUN – A hit that allows the batter to reach home plate safely. Almost always, the ball is hit out of the field of play.

MINOR LEAGUE – A group of professional teams in a league below the major leagues.

MVP – Most Valuable Player.

NATIONAL LEAGUE — One of the two organizations (along with the American League) that make up Major League Baseball, the highest level of professional baseball.

STANDING OVATION – Enthusiastic action from fans in which they stand while clapping and cheering.

PROSPECT – A player who shows enough ability at a young age that scouts believe he will be able to play at a higher level in the future.

SPRING TRAINING – A series of practices and games that help major-league teams get ready for the season.

WORLD SERIES – A best-of-seven series to determine the champion of Major League Baseball. It matches the AL and NL champions.

Index